# The Saddest Dog

**Story by Pamela Rushby**

**Illustrated by Pat Reynolds**

**Rigby PM Plus Chapter Books**
part of the Rigby PM Program
Emerald Level

U.S. edition © 2003 Rigby Education
A division of Reed Elsevier Inc.
1000 Hart Road
Barrington, IL 60010 - 2627
www.rigby.com

Text © 2003 Pamela Rushby
Illustrations © 2003 Thomson Learning Australia
Originally published in Australia by Thomson Learning Australia

10 9 8 7 6 5 4 3 2
07 06 05 04

The Saddest Dog
    ISBN   0 7578 4123 6

Printed in China by Midas Printing (Asia) Ltd

# Contents

# Chapter 1

# A Dog Arrives!

"There's a dog in our yard," said Mom.

Kim stopped eating her cornflakes and went to look out the kitchen window.

"Our side gate must be open," said Mom. "Do you know whose dog he is?"

"No," said Kim. She'd never seen the dog before.

He was a big white dog, with a black patch over one eye and another on his back. He was sitting under Kim's old swing set. His head was drooping.

"He doesn't look very happy," said Kim.

Mom stopped packing her briefcase and looked again. "You're right," she said. "He does look a bit sad."

Mom opened the back door gently and slowly approached the dog with her hand held out toward him. "Good dog," she said. "Where are you from, boy? There's a good dog."

The dog looked up slowly at Mom, then licked her hand.

"Well, he looks healthy enough, and he's certainly used to people. But what a sad looking dog he is!" said Mom. "He'll probably go home soon."

But the dog didn't go home. When Kim went out into the backyard to feed the cat, the dog was still sitting under the swing. The cat raised the fur on its back and hissed at the dog.

"Hello, boy," said Kim. The dog looked up. "Why don't you go on home?" The dog didn't move, but he seemed to look hopefully at the can of cat food in Kim's hand.

"Are you hungry?" said Kim. She looked in the can. She'd filled the cat's dish, but there was a little left over.

"Here you go, boy," said Kim. She scooped the remains of the cat food out, and stepped away from the dog. The dog sniffed it and took a little taste.

"Now, go on home, boy," said Kim. Then she went to get ready for school.

When Mom and Kim came out to the car to go to school, the dog was still in the yard.

"Kim," Mom said, "I hope you didn't give that dog anything to eat."

Kim nodded. "Well, I did," she said. "Just a little. He looked hungry. But he didn't eat much."

"Oh dear," said Mom. "Maybe that wasn't such a good idea. He might decide to stay if he thinks we're going to feed him."

She looked at the dog doubtfully. "I hope he's gone by the time we get home today."

He might decide to stay? Kim liked the sound of that! She'd always wanted a dog. She wouldn't mind if the dog was still there when they got home.

## Chapter 2

# *"He Can't Stay Here!"*

And he was! He was still sitting under the swing set, and still looking sad.

"Hello, boy!" said Kim. She was delighted to see the dog. But the cat wasn't very happy. Neither was Mom.

"Oh, bother!" said Mom. "That dog's still here! Now we'll have to look for his owner."

Mom began by looking on the dog's collar to see if there was a dog tag with a name and address. There was an old tag, but Mom couldn't read it because the letters had worn away.

"We'll visit the local stores first. Maybe Mr. Wilson knows someone who's lost a dog," said Mom. "We can put up a sign in his store window. Then we'll visit some houses nearby to see if anyone knows where this sad dog lives."

They spoke to many people, but no one had lost a dog.

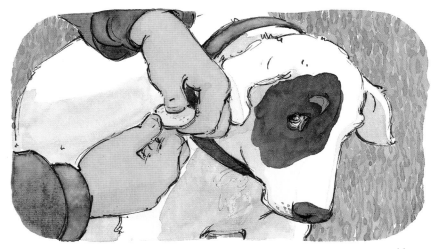

"I don't know what else to do," said Mom. "Maybe I could try phoning the local animal shelter, or the city pound. *Somebody* must own him. And I'll bet they're missing him as much as he seems to be missing them. He's a nice dog, but we don't want him to stay here!"

Kim sat down beside the dog and put
her arm around his neck. "But I do!" she
said quietly. "I want him to stay!"

Mom laughed. "Well, I can see you
want him to stay!" she said. "So he can,
but just for tonight. As soon as we find
his owners, he'll be going back to them."

*One night is better than nothing,* thought Kim. She made the dog a bed with a cardboard box and some old towels. She made a fuss of the cat so that it wouldn't feel left out. Then she found a tennis ball and tried to get the dog to play a game of fetch.

"Here, boy!" Kim called, as she threw the ball. "Catch!"

The dog wouldn't play. It sat under the swing, looking sad.

"Don't you feel like playing?" Kim asked. "What's your name? Patch? Spot? Pirate?" The dog didn't even look up as Kim listed the names. He just looked sad.

The next day, the dog was still there, under the swing. After school, Mom and Kim made signs and put them in windows at the shopping center.

"I think that should do the trick!" Mom said.

They waited that night for a telephone call. Kim hoped the phone wouldn't ring.

# Chapter 3

# *Samson?*

Two days went by, but no one phoned. It looked as if the dog might be here to stay.

"I'm not happy about this," said Mom. "A dog's a big responsibility. And they're expensive to keep. There's food and vet bills. And we've already got a cat. Frankly, Kim, we just don't have the money to spare. I'm going to have to call the animal shelter."

"Oh, no!" said Kim. "No! Please!"

After looking at Kim's pleading face, Mom gave in. "This is entirely against my better judgement," she said, "but all right, Kim. Just a few more days." She scratched behind the dog's ears. The dog looked up at her. "That's the saddest-looking dog I've ever seen!" said Mom.

Mom went into the kitchen to start fixing dinner. She turned the radio on to listen to the news. Then she called Kim.

"Kim! Could you come in and stir this for a minute while I print out my report for work tomorrow?"

"Okay," said Kim. She stood by the stove, carefully stirring the meat that was browning for a stir fry.

Kim wasn't really listening to the radio, but then she heard something that caught her attention. "… asking our listeners if they've seen a dog," the announcer said. "A dog, lost in the Hill Street area …"

Hill Street! That was only a few streets away from Kim's house! Kim stopped stirring the meat and listened carefully.

"… a large white dog with two black patches," the announcer said. "His name is Samson, and his family is really missing him. So if you've seen him, please call this station, so that we can tell his owners where he is."

Kim dropped the spoon. Stir fry was one of her favorites, but she didn't feel like eating any more. She felt rather sick.

The dog on the radio sounded just like the dog in the backyard. What if the dog really was Samson? He would have to go home. And then Kim wouldn't have a dog any more.

Mom came in holding some papers. She sniffed. "What's burning?" she said. "Oh no! Kim, stir the meat! Quick!"

Kim jumped. She grabbed the spoon and stirred the meat quickly.

"Daydreaming, were you?" said Mom. "Never mind, the meat is fine. I'll take over now."

Kim went outside and sat down beside the dog. "Are you the dog they mentioned on the radio?" she said softly. "Are you the lost dog? Are you – Samson?"

## Chapter 4

# *Doing the Right Thing*

"Samson?"

The dog's head jerked up when he heard the name. He looked eagerly around, as if he was expecting to see someone he knew. When he didn't, his head drooped, and he looked sad again.

Kim sat very still. This dog was the lost Samson, she just knew he was.

Kim knew that Samson should go back to his real family. She knew that she should tell Mom. She knew that she should phone the radio station.

But she didn't.

Another day went by. Kim tried hard to get Samson to play and to eat, but he wouldn't. Kim was getting worried.

"That dog's looking thin," Mom said. "I'm sure he's losing weight. And he's still the saddest dog I've ever seen. I hope he cheers up soon or he might …" Mom broke off. "Well, never mind."

Kim looked at the dog. Mom was right. Samson was the saddest dog she'd ever seen. She didn't want to think about what might happen if he didn't cheer up soon. She could guess it wasn't anything good.

No matter what Kim did, she couldn't make the dog happy. She knew that there was only one thing that would make him happy.

Kim took a deep breath. "I've got something to tell you, Mom."

# Chapter 5

## *Sad No More*

Mom called the radio station and told them about Samson. They passed the message on to his family. In no time at all, a car pulled up in front of Kim's house, and two children scrambled out.

The children looked eagerly into Kim's yard. "It's *him*!" they shouted. "It's really him! It's Samson! Samson! Samson!"

Samson's head jerked up. He saw the children. He leaped to his feet, rushed across the front yard, and jumped right over the fence. He jumped up at the children, licking them and barking wildly.

"Well!" said Mom. "There's no doubt about whose dog he is! Have you ever seen a happier dog?"

"No, I haven't," said Kim slowly.

She knew that she'd done the right thing. She was glad that Samson was happy again. But when Samson's family had thanked Kim and Mom, and driven away, the backyard seemed very empty.

Kim sat down on the back steps. She felt awful.

Mom sat down beside her. "Oh dear," she said. "Now Samson is the happiest dog I've ever seen. But you're the saddest girl I've ever seen. What can we do about it?"

"I don't know," said Kim.

"Well," said Mom, "why don't we to the shopping center and get some ice cream? Would that help?"

Kim loved ice cream, but she didn't think it would help the way she was feeling. But she didn't want to disappoint Mom. "I suppose it might help," she said. "Just a bit."

Mom looked at Kim thoughtfully. "You know, Kim," she said, "you did something you really didn't want to do. But you did it because it was the *right* thing to do. I know it wasn't easy. I'm so very proud of you."

Mom gave Kim a big hug.

And that helped – a lot.